T0380860

Question & Answer
Journal to Everday Living

DCS

To order additional copies of this book, contact:
Xlibris
1-888-795-4274
www.Xlibris.com
Orders@Xlibris.com

Print information available on the last page

Rev. date: 09/11/2019

Question & Answer
Journal to Everday Living

What Inspires you?

WHAT DRIVES YOU?

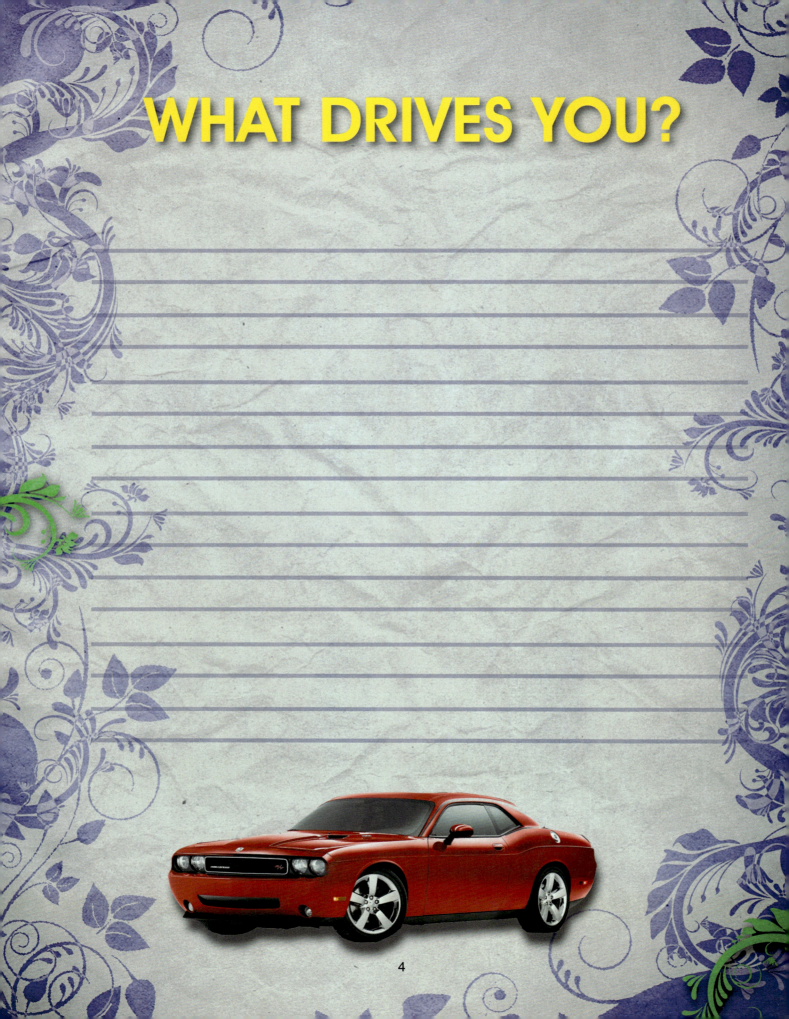

What do you Believe?

What Makes You Believe so Strongly in it?

HOw Deep Is your Love?

How do you Control Your anger? Temper?

(be quick to listen, slow to speak and slow to become angry… James 1:19-20)

EPHESIANS 4:26

How Do you Express Yourself?
(Your feelings, emotions)

How do you Feel about Gossip?

What If… List things that would happen if you were to…

What do you feel your purpose in Life is?

DO YOU KNOW WHAT GOD HAS CALLED YOU TO DO?

WHAT DO YOU THINK MAKES A GREAT GOAL?

List Your Short Term Goals:

LONG TERM:

What kind of Music do you like?

WHAT DO YOU GET OUT OF THE LYRICS AND THE RHYTHM?

HOW DO YOU FEEL ABOUT CHRISTIAN MUSIC/GOSPEL?

What do you or don't you like about Christian and when you listen to it, do you ever feel the presence of God?

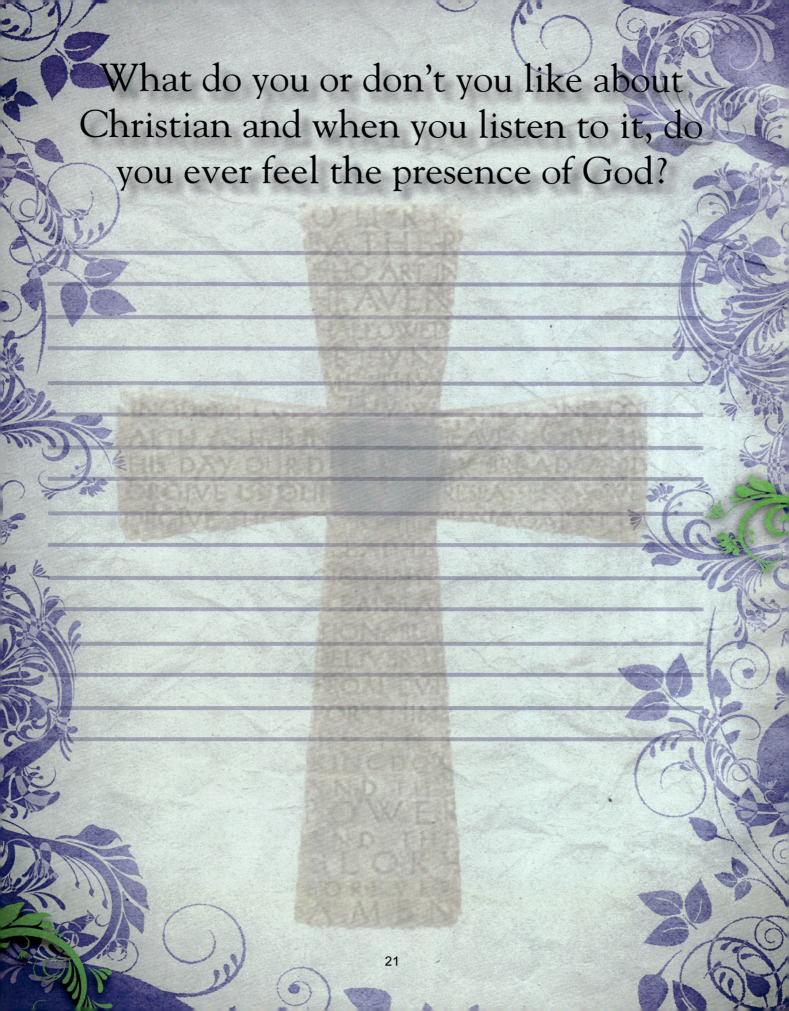

WHAT TYPE OF MOVIES AND TV SHOWS DO YOU LIKE?

What do You get out of it?

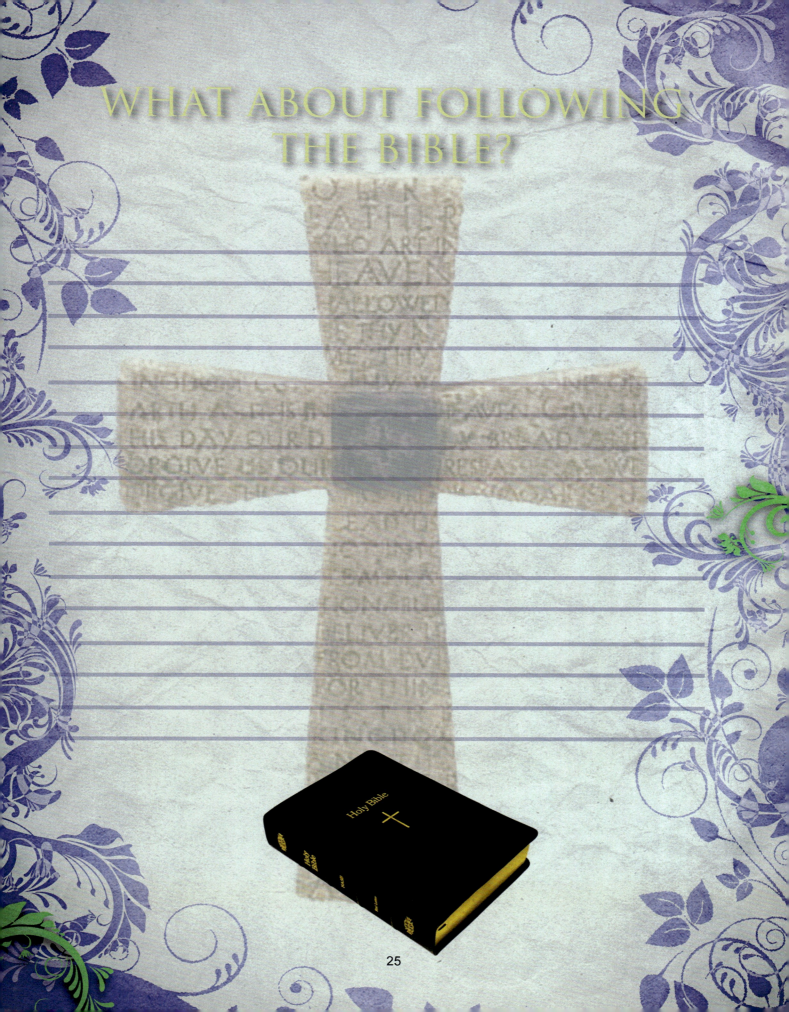

Why do you or don't you?

List Your favorite ScriPtures Here.

Printed in the United States
By Bookmasters